About t

MW00329322

Teresa was born and raised on the northwest side of Chicago to parents who emigrated from Italy. She was one of seven children. Growing up with three brothers and three sisters was both fun and challenging. Teresa was number six of the seven. Her father worked two jobs for over thirty years to put all seven kids through Catholic elementary and high school. Teresa was always very close with her parents. Watching her parents raise seven kids is where Teresa got her strong values of family and friendship.

Teresa currently lives in a suburb of Chicago. She married her high school sweetheart, Michael, and has been married for twenty years. Teresa is the mother of two teenage boys, Michael and Matthew. She teaches her sons her strong values of family and friendship in her everyday life. You will see some of the qualities come out in this book.

Author photo credit: Marla Sgarbossa

SUBURBAN CRAZY
AN EMBELLISHED TALE

TERESA WALLACE

SUBURBAN CRAZY
AN EMBELLISHED TALE

Vanguard Press

VANGUARD PAPERBACK

© Copyright 2021
Teresa Wallace

The right of Teresa Wallace to be identified as author of
this work has been asserted by her in accordance with the
Copyright, Designs and Patents Act 1988.

All Rights Reserved

No reproduction, copy or transmission of this publication
may be made without written permission.
No paragraph of this publication may be reproduced,
copied or transmitted save with the written permission of the
publisher, or in accordance with the provisions
of the Copyright Act 1956 (as amended).

Any person who commits any unauthorised act in relation to
this publication may be liable to criminal
prosecution and civil claims for damages.

A CIP catalogue record for this title is
available from the British Library.

ISBN 978 1 80016 222 8

*Vanguard Press is an imprint of
Pegasus Elliot MacKenzie Publishers Ltd.*
www.pegasuspublishers.com

First Published in 2021

**Vanguard Press
Sheraton House Castle Park
Cambridge England**

Printed & Bound in Great Britain

Dedication

To my sons, Michael and Matthew.
Always follow your dreams, no matter how crazy they
may seem.
I love you.

Italian Chaos

Growing up in a big Italian family, I love hectic. The more chaotic, the better. That will eventually change when I move. Oh God, I do not even want to say it. When I move to the suburbs... (Insert dramatic music.) So, I come from a pretty big family; there are nine of us. Yep, nine! Seven kids and two parents. When I look back, I am not sure how my mother ever did it, bless her soul. My father worked a ton (he did have to feed nine), and my mother was always with us. She should have left. Fuck, I think I would have left. We were all a pain in the ass. My poor mother. Can you imagine what she had to go through? Diapers (and we are not talking about disposable, people), breakfasts, lunches, dinners, shopping. Do you know how many pairs of socks this entailed? Man, I hate socks and pairing them up. Socks really are the most awful thing in the world. I blame my childhood. Bless her heart; I can barely handle two kids.

I grew up in a neighborhood where everyone looked out for each other. It was awesome. This taught me how to care for more than just my family. My neighborhood was a family! We played outside all day, and it was great. This all-day video gaming nonsense did not exist. It probably sucked for my older siblings as us younger kids had to always go with them. I am child six of seven. As you can imagine, this did not always sit well with the older kids. My sister was so pissed, one day she left without me, so I ran away from home. Packed a bag and headed for a better place, lol. I did not get that far because I could not cross a busy street, so they found me a block away, sucking my thumb, twirling my hair, and petting a dog in front of a fish store. This was the better place, at least the best that I could do without getting in some serious trouble. Oh, and this was not a "Let's look at the pretty fish store." This was dead fish that you buy and eat. Unless it was escargot (snails)—they were alive. I grew up in a typical ethnic Italian neighborhood. Would you expect anything less? I loved going to the fish store to shop and look. They knew my family. Of course they did—it was a small neighborhood, and everyone knew everyone. I do not know where the fucking dog came from—that is a little weird—but I was petting him like he was my own. I named him Ruffles. I did not get to keep the dog, and you will later learn I am not so big on animals either.

You will be happy to know I am no longer sucking my thumb (even though I did it to a ripe old age, possibly double digits), but I still twirl my hair. I may go fucking bald because of it—that would be a sight to see. Then my mother would be right and could say, "I told you so." Hair twirling is an attribute that drives my husband crazy. I say there could be worse. Nonetheless, it drives him crazy, and the sick part of me makes me want to do it just a little bit more.

We used to have the best water balloon fights in the neighborhood. We even had an apple tree on the block and used to get tape and tape apples together and have "apple bomb" fights with the neighborhood kids. Not going to lie; there were possible injuries. This is one of my best childhood memories. It was one of my favorite things to do. I mean, my mother had a hell of a time doing the laundry after, but I think she loved to watch us play. Can you imagine all these kids throwing apples at each other? Man, today there would be a lawsuit, restraining order, and the parent that initiated all these, BATSHIT CRAZY! I could not even imagine my mother getting a lawyer over this. Really, people are crazy today, and it is a shame. But it gives us something to talk about and make fun of, so I guess thank you, you batshit-crazy people. This is when I wish things were how they used to be. Easy, simple, and fun. People were not so uptight and nuts.

We were always together, and there were a ton of us. We played ghost in the graveyard, tag, dodgeball, wallball, running bases, freeze tag. You know, all those simple, fun childhood games. Even hiding on people's roofs. Nowadays, roof climbing is unacceptable and politically incorrect. Okay, maybe not politically incorrect, but we would need to bubble wrap our kids first. This would be acceptable for roof climbing, ha-ha. Now a monitored climbing wall. Well, you are stupid. These were the best days of our lives. See how wonderful city life was? Now I must deal with asshole parents thinking their kid is so fucking wonderful and cannot do anything wrong! Where the fuck, did they grow up? A delusional compound? Ugh. I love the city!

Let me explain city Italian life and growing up Italian. (I should let you know that the neighborhood was Italian and Irish. Hence, I married a man that is half and half… although I still have the upper hand as that would make my kids seventy-five percent Italian). Maybe this will explain all my quirks as a suburban adult, or maybe this will explain why I think everyone is an asshole. Do not take offense (which is what the world has come to—everyone being offended); I am an asshole as well. I take full ownership of being an asshole. Do you feel better? It is socially acceptable to call someone an asshole if you too agree that you are an asshole as well. Right? Hell, sometimes I am called crazy, but people seem to fail to mention that I am crazy because you are probably a fucking asshole. Are you offended I used a swear or curse word in the book? Well, stop reading now because there are a fucking lot of swear words. That is my public service announcement to you. You are welcome. And look in the mirror because you are probably an asshole! We all are. It really is in our nature to be. Accept it and move on.

Okay, so let me first talk about being left-handed. Oh, dear God, do an exorcism on this child! Yep, a left-handed Italian. The pope might have been called. "Get her to use her right hand," they would say. There are pros and cons to this. When I grew up, there were not really left-handed scissors (especially in a Catholic school). Okay, not too bad; I learned to cut righty. This will prove useful as I get older. No such thing as a left-handed desk. Okay, this is difficult but doable. I mean, what assholes could not give a proper desk because there was only one left-handed desk, and it was taken. I should have started a left-handed club. Fucking assholes! Nowadays, I bet I would get them to scream discrimination against left-handed people. Really anything but let us stay focused. It was great for sports. Although I play baseball like a righty, basketball works in my favor as most people cannot defend a lefty. You know what it sucks for? Your grandmother or nonna calling you the devil's child. That's right, ladies and gentlemen, I am a spawn of the devil because I am left-handed, and the devil is left-handed. I am not sure how they know this. Did they meet Lucifer?

Side note: It creeps me out when parents name their kid Lucifer. Really? Out of all the names, that is what you choose? You are an asshole. This is a prime example of a moment in your life where you chose to be a complete dick.

If someone can let me know where in the Bible it says Satan was left-handed, that would be great. I have the horns and all. Now, now, do not get crazy and start sending me Bible quotes about the left-handed devil. I do not care, and this is a book. Half real and half made up. Moral of the story: Not everything needs proof. At least I do not care, so thank you. Do you see green vomit coming from my mouth and my head spinning? Shit, I just peed in the hallway (having kids will do that). I mean, what the fuck! Try dealing with that growing up. Do not worry; I will not grow up emotionally hurt. I am a badass. I really do not take offense too much, plus I loved my nonna—crazy old lady. How can you even say such a thing? I remember my mother telling me a story—yelling at her, saying that she better never call me the devil again or else. I mean, why would you say that to a kid that you think is part devil? Don't you know I could fuck your shit up? My mom was a badass. She taught me how to be a badass, and I thank her for that. Don't get me wrong, my nonna was wonderful, and I loved her, and I know she loved me (she did used to bring me my own bag of Kisses). Fuck, I loved those chocolatey bags of goodness. Favorite candy till this day. I am not one of those fucking idiots that get so offended because of something or are emotionally scarred for life. She was taught something and believed it. Stand by your conviction! I mean, was it correct information? No, but live and learn, and if you do not, then you are the fucking idiot. Offended yet? We are moving on. (Just for your information: Moment the movie *The Exorcist* scared the shit out of me... till this day, that is the one movie that haunts me. The scariest movie ever for me.)

Six brothers and sisters. Six people I love so much. Six people that drive me crazy. See the above reference. I am crazy because they are assholes. Three brothers, three sisters, and a partridge in a pear tree. Just kidding about the tree and the partridge. When we were all together going into a place, we were called "the gang." Some people were upset at how big we were. Can you imagine? Are they crazy? Nope, just assholes. Yes, we planned a gang. My mother and father were like, "Let us be broke, work hard and struggle till the day we die so we can have a gang." It was all planned out. The perfect plan. They wrote it out and came up with a plan, and they succeeded. You are stupid! When you are reading this out loud, it sounds like nonsense. But I swear, people, this was true. The absurdity is not lost. We are family, you moron! People are assholes. Learn it now. The world can be a great place, and then sometimes it just sucks because, why? People! I kind of hate people. Maybe let us just say I am not a people person. We are all so different from each other. I, of course, am the better of them all, the best. Can you believe I said that? Well, it is my book, so what am I supposed to say, so-and-so is better than me? I think not. Seems pretty arrogant, and honestly, I am okay with that. I am sure someone will take offense to this, someone always does, but again, I do not care.

I have a ton of fond memories growing up. Let's' see. One time my brother helped me hide in the closet but then forgot he put me there and left. I thought I was going to die in there (okay, not really). It was hot, and I had to squeeze out of a little area because there was a mattress blocking the door. Good thing I was skinny. I would read books in there, color and draw. It was my quiet space. Mine and mine alone. I did not have to share it. It was perfect. Damn, I should go back there for some one-on-one alone time. My quiet place, my happy place. Really it was the only spot that I could be alone with my own thoughts, my own voice.

I once got pissed at my brother and put his weight set (who did he think he was, Lou Ferrigno?) in buckets of water. That took forever to do that project. I carried all those weights from the attic to the backyard. Four flights of stairs, down the driveway! Exhausting but well worth it to see his face. I thought he was going to kill me. Good thing our parents taught us never to put our hands on another human being because I do not think this would have panned out well for me. Remember he lifted, so he looked like the Hulk, right? Yes, and I work out and look like a body builder. Oh my, I am laughing so hard. What kind of person puts in so much effort to piss off their brother? I will tell you, a crazy asshole. Yes, here I am, front and center. This was a good one. I am still impressed with myself.

My one sibling failed History class, and my brother and I sang the song "What a Wonderful World," so my mother chased us out of the house. We could not come back for a couple of hours and laughed hysterically the whole time. Damn, my mom runs fast. Who in the hell is she? Jackie Joyner? I mean, she did a five-second two-mile sprint! Never underestimate a pissed off mom. Lesson learned. The youngest kid always gets away with the most shit, and here we are. If I would have failed a class, holy shit. The heavens would have opened, and the end of the world would have begun.

My older sister and I "silent fought" because my mom threatened us if we woke up my poor dad, who worked long hours and so hard—he needed his sleep. He also worked three jobs.

I made her pass out. It all started when we were getting ready to go out, and well, I think I called her a slut or a whore. I do not even remember. She came at me like a crazed, rabid animal. She could have been foaming at the mouth. I had to defend myself. I had to think fast and pull out my best WWE moves. So, I pulled my best Kerry Von Erich (wrestling person) and put her in a headlock. I got in trouble, and my defense was she passed out, so there was no screaming, and we did not wake Dad up. My mom and brother laughed, and then I got in trouble. She said it was a good point that my dad did not wake up but too bad. Damn. My mother always listened to our reasoning for doing something. But whether we were right or wrong, it did not matter. What she said goes.

There was the time when my brother's and I stuffed a snowsuit with pillows and called my sister into the dark attic (my brother's' rooms were up there) and then dropped it down the stairs on her. Ha-ha. She ran and screamed so loud. We thought we were all getting into trouble, and we did, but after, my wonderful, funny mother, who appreciated a good joke or a good prank, laughed. Man, did we get yelled at after. We were not some of those kids that got hit. She was a yeller, though.

My fondest memory revolved around a joke. My mother's favorite joke. There was a parrot in a basement, and there was a crucifix. The parrot says to Jesus, "Hey, INRI." INRI is at the top of a cross for all you atheists out there. There is more to the joke, but my mother could not get past that the parrot was calling Jesus "INRI" and she was laughing hysterically. She was belly laughing. After all these years, I still do not know the rest of the joke. I can see her laughing in my memories. I hope I never lose that.

Then there was the time at one of our weekend family picnics in our backyard that a water balloon or hose or water bucket fight started. So, who participated? That is right, my mom, and guess who else? Her mom, my other nonna. I mean, hello, so AWESOME. Well, it was awesome until my nonna fell and bruised one whole side of her body, but she took it like a champ because why? Can you say BADASS? I come from a long line of badasses. Both my nonna's were awesome, and so was my mother. The three of them could kick your ass or at least throw a shoe with such precision. I really think shoe-throwing should be an Olympic event.

We were any typical family, fighting with each other, laughing, crying together, and what have you. Till this day, we are all close. They all drive me crazy, but I love them to pieces. Our family has, of course, expanded over the years, just adding to all the crazy, just adding to the assholes. I love every minute of it and would not trade it for the world. Assholes Unite! The gang has gotten bigger.

All our friends were intermingled in each other's lives. Like I said before, everyone looked out for each other and everyone's kid brother or sister. It was so nice. There was no gossiping or being mean or acting like you were better than, or thinking your kid does no wrong. Parents all parented kids whether it was their kid or not. I wish it were like this today. God forbid that happens in the suburbs. Do not look, talk, correct or watch someone else's kid. Well, asshole, then pay attention to your fucking kid! I hate the suburbs. We all came from hardworking blue-collar parents. Your house size did not matter; your car did not matter. It is not the same, so sad. I will touch on this later, I am sure.

My first, very first car was a 1976 Chevrolet Nova (perfect, I was born that year, so funny). What was the catch? Well, besides the shit-brown color, you put the key in the ignition and turned and… nothing. Fuck! Grab the bat, hit the starter, and *vroom vroom* off I go. The best three hundred dollars I ever spent. It was a great little car for a year. I mean, it did not have any air or anything fancy, but it got me where I wanted to go. That is until the brakes went out. My quick thinking got me to pull the emergency brake. So long, first car! I will miss you and your quirky ways.

Granted, it was a little awkward trying to leave a gentleman's house at four in the morning. I know what you are thinking—*slut*. Well, I was twenty-two, and do not worry, he still married me, and now I drive a fucking minivan. I hate the suburbs. Not much of an upgrade now, is it? Do you feel bad for me yet? Fucking suburbs! I loved city life. Oh, and just to let you know, when I say city, it is not city-city but outskirt city. Do you feel bad now judging me? See, asshole. Everyone is. What else could you ask for? It was perfect. We were alike. Brought up the same way, same morals, and same ethics. Being from a family of seven, you wanted to get the fuck out—I am not going to lie. My husband says that I would live in a compound with my family if I could. He is right; I totally would.

I got my first apartment with a friend's friend. Did we know each other, you ask? Nope. Not one bit. She was Italian, I was Italian, and what else do you need? Trust from the beginning. Italians are no rats and are good people. If you happen to be Italian and are a rat or not a good family person, then maybe you should get your lineage checked. We had the best roach-infested apartment ever. We hung sheets to keep the air in a room so it would be cold in the summer months (we only had one air unit). We went out together and partied. Okay, I really did not party. I was and am a prude. She partied and wore cute outfits. A little jealous she had a life, and I did not, but that is okay; it was my choice. I was a lame loser. Such a dork. One night she took me to a bar. At the bar, a girl walks up to me and grabs my boob—*um, hello*—and walks away. I was in such shock when my friend walked up to me—she said I looked like I had seen a ghost and asked what was wrong. When I explained what happened, she laughed. I laughed (uncomfortable), and we went home. Hello, asshole. Nowadays, I am always looking for someone to cop a feel on me, ha-ha. I chose to just hang at neighborhood bars from then on. You know the ones where people know your name and look out for you. It was like *Cheers* but without the cameras. The wonderful city neighborhood bar. I love you, city! There were good people there. No pressure, and safe.

Our first night in the apartment together, I got a really bad allergic reaction to a tanning bed and spent the night naked in the bathtub with cold water running over me. Not knowing what it was, my roommate— *Hello, please come see my naked fat ass and help me*— took me to the emergency room. What a sweet girl. I am sure this is the last thing she wanted to do, but this is what roommates are for. Can you say embarrassing? Welcome to the apartment! The next week she had gotten a belly button ring and decided to zip it in her pants. I was straddling her to try to get it out. That would have been a sight to see. We liked to keep things spicy. The third week her air conditioner had a spider infestation, and her room was covered. Commence, big bear, little bear. Good thing we got to know each other before we moved in together—yeah, right. This is real life, people, not a sitcom. I do not think a writer could come up with this shit.

The next two years would be glorious, filled with awesome memories. From the pulled muscle not even making it out of the stairwell for our run, to the gas leak with the neighbor lighting a cigarette over said gas leak. To this day, we are good friends and will always be. I mean, hello, we saw each other naked. Who would not want to stay friends with this hot piece of ass? This is true friendship for life. A no-judgment friendship.

When I moved into the apartment, it was extremely hard on my parents as you did not do things like this until you were married (remember, old school Italian). They barely talked to me, which does not make sense either. But all was good. They understood I was not like the other six. Remember, I was the best, not an asshole. I feel bad—what I put my parents through! Two wonderful, glorious years were spent in that apartment, and then I get engaged. Can you fucking believe it? ENGAGED! (Insert celebration music here.) You cannot always get the milk for free; sometimes you must just buy the cow. I looked like shit the day he proposed. I came from work, was running late for dinner, so I threw my hair into a ponytail. If I could do it over, I would. The lesson here is always look good because you never know what is going to happen. Usually they say, like, "Always leave the house with clean underwear," or something in case you get in a car wreck. Well, unless you are married, always leave the house done up in case you get engaged; that is my advice to you. I never did learn from this lesson because I look like shit most of the time.

"You are wonderful... I want to spend the rest of my life with you..." Yadda, yadda. I am engaged, and it is forever. Do you know why I know it is forever? Because it is cheaper to keep her! HA!

Confirmation: holy hair

First
Communion:
the left handed
devil gets
blessed

Mom's kitchen

Where the family parties took placed

The traditional Italian Easter egg

City living

Baby picture

Next to the radio

Yes, my ears are pierced

Married Life

I am moving out of the apartment and into my very own house. I am so excited. I am staying in the city because I love the city. I do work in the 'burbs, but who gives a fuck. City is where it is at and near my old neighborhood, even better. Family is near, check! Friends are close, check! Thank you, thank you, thank you. My man, my man, my man is wonderful.

We actually met when I was sixteen. He got knocked the fuck out! Literally. I accidentally knocked him the fuck out. If you ask him, I am sure he would recount the encounter completely differently. But he got knocked the fuck out. I met him in the woods where kids would go and drink and smoke and do stupid shit. Of course, this was all illegal. I mean, not me. My kids are going to eventually read this book someday. So, for my boys, your father and I went to hang with our friends and tried to guide these hooligans to change their ways and be better people. Okay, now back to reality. You just must run faster than the slowest person, or else when the cops came, you would get caught. I was fast! Must have gotten my running skills from my mom. The first time I went to the woods, I was a little nervous. Did I mention I was a prude? Oh my God, I never did anything wrong. I think I had my first drink when I was twenty-one. What a loser! The friends we were meeting were playing a stupid tag game of some sort. Yes, we were immature. I was just walking up, and BAM! Sorry, but the fucker was running at me. Why? To kill me? Attack me? How the fuck was I supposed to know that they are idiots. I just left and did not come back for like a month. Our next encounter was an introduction, as I was the one that hit him. Well, thank you very much. Fucking rat! The guy that told him was Irish, not Italian. He obviously does not know about the rat code. That was it. He fell in love with me. Could you blame him? I am fucking perfect. P-E-R-F-E-C-T. What else could he ask for? Beautiful, check. Awesome body, check. Smart, check. Naive, check! Who would not want to get with this? I am fucking perfection! (Do I have you laughing yet? I am laughing typing this.) Nowadays, I am what you call a MILF (Mother I'd Like to Fuck). Nah, just kidding, but it's suburban life now, so what the fuck, why not? So here we go.

We are in the house. It is a beautiful Georgian in the city. I love it. I love the city. It's three blocks from his parents—fucking momma's' boy. I mean, who the hell moves this close to their mom? A momma's boy, that is who! We finally move in together after we get back from our honeymoon. That was awesome and fun and, oh my God, it was sex, sex, sex! Perfect. Which on the way to the airport, he asked if he could just go take a nap with his pillows in his bed. Where? At his mother's house! Fucking momma's boy. Now, I am not a bitch but remember—it is cheaper to keep her. I am sure he was joking, sort of. He took a nap at our new house. That is what I thought (I am a badass). So, we are getting to know each other. It is a learning period. He thinks I should cook more. (I eventually become a good cook, but that is when I become a suburbanite.) I think he should fix more shit. I was wrong. He did not learn shit. He should have had a sticker on him that read: *"DOES NOT KNOW HOW TO FIX THINGS AND DOES NOT OWN A TOOLBOX. PLEASE CALL HANDY MAN."* Fixing up house lesson 101: DO NOT, I repeat, DO NOT leave husband in house alone during a DIY project. Let me write out the scene for you.

We had just gotten done with sanding the walls. We are going to paint them ourselves. Just a side note: If you are ever thinking of doing this, do not. Hire someone. You will spend more money and time than it's worth. Okay, back to the story. My hubby is hungry, so I am going to run out to get food. This was my first mistake. I should have ordered. Never leave your husband home alone. I cannot stress this enough. We need to finish painting today as the carpet is being laid the next day. Poor timing skills on our part. Another side note: Give yourself a day in between, just in case. When I come back from getting food, I walk in through the front door and can't see a thing. Not a damn fucking thing! Is this a fucking joke? Asshole. What the fuck happened? I was gone ten minutes. Clouds of dust billowed around me. I could not see anything. My genius husband got a great idea (maybe he should read more). As a present, he got a leaf blower. Are you with me, people? Do you see where this is going? Yes, a leaf blower. So, Einstein decided to blow the dust out of the house. I apologize to Einstein here because I am now insulting Einstein. There was a mini-tornado of dust in my house. It took hours for it to settle. I cried. My eyes burned. I called my brother-in-law and sister to help. I cried. I mean, what the fuck. College graduate, huh? I want to see the diploma. It was so awful. We had to let the dust settle before we could begin wiping down everything with wet rags and use a vacuum cleaner. It was a long, long night. He is lucky I stayed with him. No judge in the world would have sided with him. I think if you go back into this house all these years later, there is probably still dust settling.

We soon got the carpeting in, and that is where the first lie of my marriage came in. (You will be happy to know it was my only lie, but it was needed.) So, I rinsed out the paintbrushes in the basement sink. I forgot to clear out the sink (I did not know that I needed to), and the paint clogged up the drain. When I went to go to the laundry, all the water spilled over from the sink onto MY NEW RUG! That is right, fuck, fuck, fuck! OMG, I am such an asshole. Commence Operation Bullshit.

"Hey, hun, just want to let you know that when you cleaned all the paintbrushes, you forgot to clean the sink, and there is water everywhere. Have fun cleaning it up."

So that was that. I am a fucking awful person. I should have been like, "Oh, well, the fucking house had a tornado in it." But did I? No! I was worried he would be upset with me. Stupid little girl I was. Now, if you ask me, who the fuck cares. All is good, we are wonderful and have a wonderful life. I so love my husband. You are going to get sick of me writing this and you reading this. Do not be so fucking judgmental or jealous. If you need to refer to being an asshole, see Italian Chaos.

Our first garage break-in actually went pretty smooth as well. Firstly, other than a lawn mower, we owned nothing else that would need to be out in a garage. Not one single tool. At least not one big enough to keep in a garage. So, it is around two a.m., and the bell rings, and there is a knock at our door. I wake my husband (who could actually sleep through a robbery), and he finally goes downstairs.

"Who is it?"

"Your neighbor's friend. I am a cop, and it looks like your garage got broken into."

I guess my husband felt safe enough. He opens the door. There stands a '''six-foot-three man with a spotlight.

"Hey, it looks like your garage got broken into. You may want to check it out."

So, in the next thirty seconds, I do not know what happens or if the guy got a look at my man, who is super sexy but honestly, never played a lick of football and is maybe one hundred and sixty-five soaking wet, but all of a sudden, the cop says, "You know what, I will go look for you. Stay here."

HA. Not that I want my husband to go out there, hell no, the cop is trained, and my loving, wonderful hubby is not, but it is a good story—exaggerated, like all my other stories, but good.

Let us talk about my hubby for a minute. What else could I ask for? He is a wonderful, wonderful man. Honest, loving, and has stood by my side in the best and worst of times. I could not ask for a more awesome husband. I love you, babe. Are you jealous yet? You should be because I got the best of the best. Okay, enough of all the sentimental stuff.

Living as a young married couple is great. Of course, you had to get used to it. There was always that friend that was rude. He would call and say shit like, "Get your husband." Not a "hello," not a "how are you?" Fuck that! He realized he needed to play nice after I kept hanging up on him. Fucking dick! You want to act like a bitch, well, so can I—bring it on!

I have fond memories of my first home. My hubby went out one night downtown. Me and my bestie went out and were drinking. She got a ride home, and so did I. Since we were both bored, we decided to tell her mother (who did not like to drive) that my husband was out of town (um… it was supposed to be downtown, and he would be back that night). I said I was afraid and asked if she could please drive my bestie to me. Man, we were assholes. She did, in the snow and all. I love her! See, moms do that shit for their kids no matter what age. We proceeded to finish off a case of beer, and when my husband called, he said he would pick up food. *Oh yeah! We are going to get food. I am so hungry*. When he got back home, he was pissed to find out we'd ordered eighty-five dollars' worth of saganaki! OPA! It was the best night. We were assholes, and it was awesome. I love my city friends. They are normal and no drama. You can say fuck off but kiss each other the next day and break bread. These suburban folks are fucking touchy, offended, fucking morons.

Yes, owning a home was fun, especially after I Pledged the floor (oopsie, I did not know I was not supposed to do that), and my husband went sliding across the floor, crashing into the wall. Always an exciting day. Keep life spicy, I say. Simple and normal is what I like.

Well, it is time. We are planning on expanding our brood. A long discussion pursues, and we are off, looking at buying in the 'burbs. God help me. My kid is going to grow up in a 'burb! They wear bicycle helmets, right? Safety first. They go to public schools, right? Are there streetlights? Cul-de-sacs? Coyotes? Well, the search is on. We end up finding a place and sell our house and go to close on it. FUCK! The sellers are backing out at closing. Are you fucking kidding me? Damn suburbanites, you suck! You know where I must go to now? My in-laws' house. That is right. This should be fun. I mean, who would not want to live with their in-laws? I mean, let's try to procreate in your parents' house. Silent sex is so romantic. I mean, I know we pulled this shit when we were not married, but now, well, it is just awkward.

Well, my hubby got his way; he is now back with his mommy. She reads him books at night and tucks him in. Okay, I am just kidding, but it's funny shit, right? We find a house. He loves it, and I hate it. This is what married couples do. I say red, he says green. I say left, he says right. It is a rite of passage. It is in the marriage handbook—look it up. Man, there should have been a handbook or maybe a crystal ball, even better.

Suburbia Here We Come

We will soon learn in the years to come that it will be a thorn in our side. This fucking suburban house! I think it is possessed or never wants us to leave as owners. Like never ever. We find a 1926 Victorian. We start doing some work on it. All hired work, of course—I learned my lesson. Pull a radiator here, paint there, caulk here, done. We build this wonderful back porch that extends the length of the back of the house. It was so beautiful and big. I loved it, or at least I learn to love it.

I come home from work one night, and my husband thought it would be funny to watch me put away groceries with his face pressed against the back window. I was not used to the deck reaching this window. What he thought was a funny moment would prove to be a not-so-funny moment. Asshole. When I realized it was him, it was already too late. Fucker does not know what he is in for. I grab a butcher knife, start screaming and head for the upstairs. He came through the house screaming, "Tre, Tre, it's me, it's me." I was upstairs going through the window, ready to jump on my neighbor's roof. Yes, I had it all planned out in the event someone broke in. I know, psychopath that I am. This proves my theory I am crazy because you are an asshole. My whole life, I always planned the "what would you do moment" in my head. I always had to be prepared. Hey, you can never be too careful. I watch scary movies; bitches always die going out the front door. I keep a ski mask in my nightstand just in case someone breaks in just so I can put it on and be like, "What the fuck? I was here first." My husband thinks I am crazy. I do not even know how he stays with me. Oh yes, I forgot, I am a hot piece of ass. My poor husband, I feel so bad he has to put up with my shit. But again, it is in the marriage handbook. How great would that be if there was an actual handbook? Genius!

We proceed to clear out the house and make it how we want it prior to moving in. Pull old radiators, check! Paint every room, check! Remove weird jar with possible snakeskin or something fucking crazy that you only see in the suburbs, check! Remove beautiful old oak tree in front of my home that I love, but it's dead, check... hold up... raccoon family in it and neighbor saves and relocates wild animals, fuck! Okay, I should have known that this was an omen. Nothing is ever easy. I mean, what? You do what? I never even heard of such a thing, but yeah, I guess that is a job. Okay, so now what? So, I have to call the tree people and let them know that they cannot touch the tree for a week because I need to relocate a raccoon family that has been living in the tree for years. Fuck! Fuck! Fuck!

How do you relocate raccoons? Do you get an eviction notice for animals? I mean, is there a Craigslist of some sort for this kind of shit? I mean, really! Fuck, where did I move to? The situation gets worse. I did not think it could, but it actually does. Okay, now I am completely and utterly fucked! I can never leave my house again or talk to my wonderful animal rescue neighbor because they came at seven a.m. and cut the tree down. Are you kidding me? *Hello, did you not listen to me when I told you not to fucking come!* Oh God, why? I mean, first, did the raccoons get out? Were they cut up into a billion little pieces? Did the neighbor chain herself to the tree? I do not even want to look outside. I guess I am the asshole now. Perfect way to start out with the neighbors. I avoid the neighbor for like two weeks, and then I decide I must be a grown-up and go talk to her and apologize, right? Would you do that? Ugh, I hate this shit. Yes, I am sorry the dumb fuck did not follow directions and killed your raccoon family. (They did get out.) I cannot believe I have to go talk about this. UGH, I hate the suburbs! I am on my way, walking over, and my cell phone rings. Perfect, this will delay me by what? Five minutes?

"Hello."

"Well, err, um, this is erm, Rocky Raccoon, and today I went, erm, for a paper and came back and well... what did you do with my family? Well, I'm gonna get you, gonna get you good."

I've never laughed so hard. I think I may have or may not have just peed my pants. Asshole. I had to run back into my house because I could not stop laughing, and the neighbor was about to come outside. I could not even compose myself (plus, yep, I peed my pants). I received messages like this all day. See, people, this is why I love my family. I was actually upset about it, but they teased me. I fucking love my family.

The next day I do go speak to the neighbor. I am a grown-up and part asshole. She had removed the raccoon family the night before (thank goodness), and all was well. The Earth started spinning again. This will be the first encounter with my neighbor that maybe why we did not hit it off so great. We ended up becoming friends. I told her that I would marry her one day because I needed her to remove dead animals from under my porch, kill massive bugs for me, catch a mouse, and help me plant. I do not do any of this, and I am okay with it. Domestic Goddess, yes, Nature whisperer, not quite.

Once she tried to convince me to go camping with her. That was pretty funny, me... camping. *Hello, I cannot even kill a spider.* Fishing, lighting a fire, smelling like a fire, sleeping… What? In a tent? Peeing outside? Are you fucking crazy? No, thank you. Me and nature and animals do not mix. They are out to get me. I mean, Wisconsin Dells is roughing it for me. Even then, I bring my own sheets, blankets, pillows, and towels to a hotel. Can you imagine me camping? HA! Oh wait, and soft toilet paper because come on, who does not like their ass wiped with gentleness? Maybe assholes do not? The alternative would be your finger popping out at a very inopportune time. Do you know how many times you would have to wash your hands to get that smell out? Then there is the whole hygiene issue. I need to shower every day and smell pretty and feel clean all over. Anything less for me would be torture. I do not know how girls do not wash their hair every day. I would be like an oil slick. It is the Italian in me. If I did not get to shave, I would look like Chewbacca. Again, the Italian in me. Trust me; you do not want me to look like that—it would be awful. I would be able to braid that shit.

They were a nice family that lived next to me. I mean "nice"—I had the cops called on me twice, but it really was not my fault, and they were good people. Let us call those situations misjudgments on their part. I always give people the benefit of the doubt. But on a side note, if you call the police on neighbors, you are a pussy. A furry fucking pussy! Who lives like that?

Animals. We are not animals. I am not an animal. Knock on my door. Discuss the situation. Let us agree or disagree and do what we were born to do, dislike each other in private and talk behind each other's backs. Problem solved. You go about your business, and I go about mine. Moral: Mind your own business, people. See, you learned something.

Suburban Life

So here I am—suburban life. My first night here, I cried. I actually cried for three months. I hate it here. I hate it here. I hate it here. Do you get the point? I can keep repeating it to myself, but it does not make it untrue. Fuck you, suburbs! It is quiet and there are so many wild animals. What the fuck. You can hear them at night; they are watching me. I am fresh meat to them. They torment me, till this day. In my mailbox today was a village handout regarding garbage and coyotes. I mean, COYOTES! I did not think it was true. Oh, it is true. Where the hell am I? I never actually saw a coyote until I moved here. You might as well have told me it was a unicorn. Only saw this shit on National Geographic. At least growing up in the city, there were streetlights, actual streetlights, actual sidewalks, actual curbs. I swear if I see a horse and buggy go down the street, I am going to lose my shit. Oh my GOD, oh my GOD, where did I move to? I want to go back home. My home, not back with my in-laws; I mean, let us not get crazy.

Quiet sex still haunts me. This is NOT home, at least not yet. It was much simpler where I used to live.

Everyone knew you. I was so-and-so's kid sister. Leave her alone or else get the wrath of the neighborhood boys. Not to mention her brothers. It was nice. Everyone knew each other, everyone was kind, and everyone grew up with the same parenting style. It is not the same here. This self-righteous, my-kid-can-do-no-wrong mentality, is mean and lies to get what they want, and the dumb parents buy it. Well, that is just disgusting. Fucking assholes. These parents are so dumb. I think I am a dumb parent too or could turn into a dumb parent. Shit, holding breath. Okay, so now I am here, now what? I need to adapt. Survival of the fittest, right? I am not moving back, even though I would love to move back. *Maybe I can move back*, I think. I am delirious. My best friends are there, you know, in the "old neighborhood" or the "city" as I call it. So, what if it is the northwest side of Chicago—dammit—my zip code was Chicago. Oh, how I loved it and did not really appreciate it. Bring me back! I am sorry, can I get a do-over? Okay, I am dealing with this head-on. I mean, it is not therapy-worthy, but still.

"Go outside!" That is what my head is telling me. *"Go venture out." "Get in your car and drive around."*

I cannot. What if I get lost? I surely will not find my way back. The "blocks" out here are not city blocks. They curve and round and go on forever, and then just when you think you have found your way, there is a dead-end! Are you fucking kidding me? A dead end, really? I need GPS just to get through my neighborhood. Walking GPS app is the best. Trust me, it helps. Yes, I got lost walking. Stupid suburbs.

So, I am going to do this—suburban mall, here I come. It supposedly has everything, not like the one main department store my mall had. I chicken out and head back to my Northwest Chicago mall, (which is in another suburb but right across from my old zip code, so close enough). Here I am driving back to the "city." A twenty-minute drive. Well, to a Chicagoan, everything is twenty minutes. Ahh, that was wonderful—my happy place. I am back home now, ugh. My happy place is gone.

It starts raining, downpour. Why don't I remember such rain in the city? Was I just oblivious? Did I just not care? I mean, I know streets flooded, but it just seemed okay. My husband is at a ball game or something, and here I am alone in this big house. Big, scary, probably haunted house. For sure, someone was murdered in this house. I know it. I should look it up. There is probably some dead body buried in the basement from long ago or in the walls. Do you think it's a nice ghost? A little girl? An old man? Maybe a woman dressed in an old Victorian gown? Fuck, why did I do that? I am scared shitless now. Someone is watching me. Who? Is the ghost going to attack me? I hate scary movies. If shit starts flying off the wall, that is my line in the sand. I am out. But where am I going? Sit my ass back down.

I do not feel like cleaning, so I might as well open a bottle of wine and catch up on the shows that I have taped. I love wine. Hello Mr. Joel Gott. You taste yummy. Oh, and you perv, that is the name of the wine. Man, it's getting really dark outside."

Knock at the door.

Oh, come on, I am scared shitless enough.

"Hello, who is it?"

I do not want to look out the window and check. What if it is a killer and they shoot me through the door? Will they try to knock the door down? Back at my city home, my neighbor was a cop. It was nice. I felt safe. I had four cops on my block and two firemen. Lucky me. What else could I have asked for? I felt safe and protected. My badass block. Okay, back to the ominous knock.

"Hey, Teresa, it's your neighbor Janet."

I open the door, and she has a flashlight. *Fuck, I need to get me one of those.*

"The whole block lost power, and you are the only one with power."

Sweet. Oh shit! Do I have to invite her in now?

"Glad you answered. I thought you would be in your basement."

"Why would I be in the basement?" *My scary spidery basement, you know, where the body is buried.*

"Because of the tornado warning. Aren't you watching TV or listening to the radio?"

A FUCKING WHAT? You guys (that's city talk) get tornados?

"I was watching recorded shows. Haven't heard anything, and Mike is at a game."

"Well, the power will probably go out soon."

"I don't have a flashlight or anything. What do I do?"

Damsel in distress! Please come save me because I have no idea what I am doing because I am from the city, and this is now the closest I have come to camping.

"Here, take mine. I am right next door if you need anything. Just wanted to check on you."

Okay, so I am a pussy. That is right, a certifiable pussy. Granted, I did not know anything about the tornado warning, but I guarantee you I would not have left my house if I did to check on my neighbor. Selfish, scary cat bitch that I am. Now we are talking tornados! I've seen them on TV, in movies, on news reports when they touch down and destroy towns and people's lives so horrifically. Now I am supposed to deal with this shit. There is not enough wine in the world right now. I grab pillows and blankets and head to my basement. I do not forget my wine and make me a platter of cheese and crackers. I got time, right? A girl must eat. And what if I got stuck down there? What if it's days and I do not get to eat because I am trapped now in my basement for days with no food or drink and must survive on wine and cheese and crackers? My sole companions are a corpse, spiders, and a ghost. Definitely a cheese platter, oh, and I will grab a blanket. Me and my kids are supposed to go hungry. Wait, I do not have kids yet. What if I am not found for days? I mean, if I am going to be taken by a tornado or trapped down there, I might as well have something to occupy my time. Here goes the pussy, walking to the basement—to find out we are not that far into the suburbs, and a tornado has not really ever happened where I am at. I think I was the only one that went to the basement. So embarrassing.

Let us talk about my basement. My home is an old suburban Victorian—built in 1926. It is old and beautiful and scary. If you told me there were ghosts in it or that it was possessed, I would not be surprised. I go to the basement. It is damp and moist. Yep, moist, so you know it is definitely creepy. I put some towels on the floor and sit. What should I do? Should I go to the hallway that leads to a set of about five stairs that lead nowhere or open the scary cellar door? It's like two terrible options. The Russian roulette of basements. "They probably murdered someone in there once?" *Fuck, stop trying to scare yourself.* It is a lose-lose situation. I sit and eat my cheese and crackers. *"Don't think of anything. Don't think of ghosts or demons or anything. You are just scaring yourself."*

I hate the suburbs! What happened to my fireman and cops? I was safe then, so safe. Now what do I have? Darkness, tornados, wild animals. That is no life, no life at all for me. There are probably huge spiders down here. *Please do not crawl out. Please don't crawl out.* I bet they could eat me alive. I bet I am their charcuterie board. All right, since I am down here might as well start laundry. Fucking laundry, I hate it. I mean, there are only two of us! It's like a football team lives here. *"Oh my God! It's a giant centipede. Forget it! I am going back upstairs and am not doing laundry."* I heard they mate with themselves. Is that true? If so, that is fucking cool; if not, good rumor. I cannot forget my cheese, crackers, and wine.

Scary basement part two. Or should I say two and three? Have you ever had a raccoon in your basement or how about a family of opossums? Well, I can safely say that this girl has. Yep, city girl meets animal kingdom. Stop it! I know you are jealous. Oh God, I hate the suburbs. Let us start with the opossum story. That is probably the best one to start with since it happened first.

Okay, scary basement 101: Where there's a broken window in the basement that leads to under your front porch, DO NOT ASK YOUR HUSBAND TO FIX IT! Did I not learn my lesson from the leaf blower incident? Does everyone understand that, especially if your husband is city folk like me? He will put a blanket over it with a *DO NOT ENTER* sign attached to it and tape it to the wall. People, this is no joke. Do you feel bad for me yet?

"What's that sound? It sounds like hissing." I am sitting upstairs on my couch in the TV room next to my husband.

"I don't hear anything."

"Shh, listen. You didn't hear that?"

"No, you are hearing things. It's probably the water tank or the furnace."

"Go look."

"No."

Okay, fine. I am CRAZY. Yes, I am crazy. It must be the fucking ghost. The pretend ghost in my head. Girls, listen closely. You know why you think you are crazy or feel crazy? It's because our men drive us there. The suburb is getting to me. Perfect. I am hearing shit. I am in the midst of a psychotic break. *It is nothing.* I repeat this to myself all night because, honestly, I am afraid I will be eaten alive. Mauled in the middle of the night. Woken up by something on top of me or sitting on me, staring me straight in the eyes. Bear is not out of the question. You may laugh; I am not laughing.

Morning comes, and I am about to do laundry in the basement. I am walking down the stairs. I do not think I could have walked any slower if I tried.

Watch out for hands grabbing your ankles.

What am I doing?

Stop it! Stop scaring yourself!

I walk over to the laundry part of our scary haunted basement. There is the washer, dryer, and the utility sink.

Hmm, that's odd. That looks like animal shit in the sink. Is that animal shit? I get closer. *I think that's animals' shit!*

Are you fucking serious! Are you fucking animal-shit-in-my-sink serious! I hurry up, throw laundry in, and run upstairs like I am being chased by a coyote. Why did I pause to throw laundry in? Because I think I knew the truth about what was in the basement. "That damn coyote flyer. I can't stop thinking of it.

I refuse to go into the basement. I just refuse. He can fucking go if he wants clean clothes.

"Hon, I am not going down there. I swear there is animal shit in the basement sink. Please go look."

"I don't know. I mean, it looks like shit, but I looked around, and there is nothing down there."

Well, Mr. Leaf-blower, I don't buy it, don't buy it one bit! Want to know one way to never, ever, ever, never have to go in your basement to do laundry? Make yourself fully believe that there is a wild animal in your basement. Don't just think it, really believe it. A few days later, I hear footsteps running up the basement stairs, and the door slams with a shrill of someone who has the heebie-jeebies.

Husband: "Okay, so I moved some installation that I noticed on the floor and thought why is that there, and, well, there are baby opossums in it."

So I say, "So the hissing that I heard is the mother, and now we have a family of opossums in our house, and we do not know where the mother is. She is probably going to kill most of the babies and us now because of your smell, and we have a fucking family of opossums, and who the fuck do we call for that?"

These wilderness animals SUCK, you hear me, they SUCK! Suburbia, you SUCK! Well, at least I do not have to do laundry. Glass half full, people, glass half full. So, I am fully sane, people. I am not crazy at all. I feel a little better knowing this.

We fix the basement window and put drywall up, so at least it is not so scary any more. At least for now, the cobwebs are gone. Perfect. No more animal's, right? Nope, we are in the 'burbs, people, the 'burbs.

Welcome home, raccoon family! That is what the doormat should have said. Ugh! So here we go. Fuck you, Suburbia. Fuck you! It is mating season. Well, at least the raccoons are getting frisky. I am still creeped out about the opossum. Why is this happening to us? To me? Put mothballs under your porch, fix the porch, put heavy rocks, and use ammonia rags. Well, I did it all, and you know what happened? That whore raccoon kept mating, bringing strange male raccoon after strange male raccoon home. You know that bitch was not using protection, and the last thing I needed was to house a family of raccoons. I am not raising a family of raccoons. This bitch was smart. I would wake up to a pile of the rags and mothballs and old spindles (where the hell did those come from and what is really under my porch) behind my car. All right, it is on. You are going to fuck with me; I am going to fuck with you. I am a person, for Pete's sake, and you are a raccoon. *I got this.* Nope, I do not. She crawled through my wall and ripped the drywall and installation out and made a home in my new drywalled basement. *"Are you FUCKING KIDDING ME?"* *"Dear God, I hate the suburbs. Can you hear me? I hate the suburbs."*

The horny whore of a raccoon gets relocated—to where I do not know. Maybe a sex addiction house. I really do not care. Thank goodness for coyote urine. Did I really just say that? I cannot believe it myself. First, I cannot believe that there is such a thing, and second, I can't believe I actually bought some. Raccoons scare the shit out of me. They have followed me up my front porch and sat at the screen window of the door. Not afraid at all. Fuck you, raccoon. The fear is real, people. So, my good friend coyote came to the rescue. They are not so bad. Maybe suburban life is growing on me. I got this.

Let me go for a nice run and be one with nature. FUCK! COYOTE! What the hell, it's one thirty p.m. What the hell is it doing walking around a neighborhood? Oh God, I might throw up. What do I do? Freeze, play opossum, run… oh God, I am going to die. I will be on the news: Young, Hot, Sexy Suburban Woman Gets Mauled by Coyote. Perfect, that is all I need. Great, I am wearing granny panties. My mom was right about the underwear thing. That is what everyone is going to notice. Granny fucking panties, perfect. My life is complete now. Ugh, I hate suburban life. It goes the other way. Damn thing fooled me, because now it is running at me. *"Is this fucking happening?"* I take off. I am Jackie Joyner; I am a cheetah. OMG, I think I just tinkled in my pants. Great, now it's urine-filled granny panties when they find my body. *"Did I wax?" Pull it together!* I am running into the poor little old lady's garage (she left her door open). I do not want to scare her, but fuck, that is a coyote. I bang on the door; she peeks out. I yell, "There's a coyote chasing me. Help me."

She does not let me in. She comes out. (I see she has a little doggie inside, and I am thinking, okay, if the coyote comes, I am barreling over her and throwing her dog at it.) It finally goes away. Oh, thank goodness. Seriously, I hate the suburbs. Just when I think, okay, it will be good, I am again showed why I hate it here. I make it back home safely. The husband of the kind little old lady—whose doggie I was all ready to sacrifice—comes home, and the wife must have told him because he goes looking for me to make sure I make it home okay. That is so sweet; until he finds out I almost had his dog murdered. Suburbia at its finest. In the city, that would have never, ever happened. Okay, maybe it is not so bad; give it a chance. I am home now and go to grab something from the garage. *What is that buzzing sound"?*

"Hey, hun, there is a buzzing sound in the garage, so weird." Here comes my hubby, you know, the one that ran as fast as he could from the baby opossum and shrieked. "What's that over there?"

Well, it's bees. Not the good old honeybee that we need to grow food but the nasty, nasty, I-am-going-to-torture-you-and-sting-the-shit-out-of-you bee. Not one, not two, but a fucking lot! A whole wall dedicated to bees in my garage. They have built a home. A home that welcomes all shitty non-contributing murder wasp bees. I do not care any more! It could be one bee, two, two million, a trillion. Nasty, nasty, nasty! How am I supposed to love animals when this shit is happening to me? I mean, I do not want to see any animals ever get hurt or captured, but just stay away from me. I don't understand what my attraction is. Hot? Yes. Sexy? Yes. Smart? Yes. Fine ass motherfucker? Yes. I mean, I know I am this hot piece of ass but come on, you must feel sorry for me now. This stuff does not happen to real people, at least not the same person. I am jinxed. No luck. Besides the occasional coyote in my backyard at midnight (really, no joke), the only other animals I have been in contact with are a skunk (too close for comfort) and a duck. Ducks are cute, but in my case, they are until they are not, and attack. OMG, I hope that never happens. I will turducken its ass if it ever does. My friends make fun of me when I run now and see an animal. I clap my hands and shout, "Whoo-hoo." The animals scurry off. All the stars are aligned now, so I hope not to have any more animal issues.

Oh, and as a side note of suburban life: I have no problem with domesticated animals. Except cats—they are the devil. And hamsters or gerbils, they are rodents and gross. Oh, and dogs, yuck and smelly. Okay, so maybe I have an issue with *all* animals. I love my friend's dog, but now the pit bull-type dog (they have a rap sheet) that chases a runner down and jumps on them. I don't blame the dog here. I blame the owner. First, you know your dog is a runner. Second, you know your dog is a jumper. So, is it smart to let your dog out to run the neighborhood? You, owner, are an asshole, and this is why pit bulls get a bad rap because, again, you are an asshole owner. If you think it's smart to let your dog go in the front of your house to run around, then your dog is smart, and you are fucking stupid. Good day to you, dumbass!

Running for Food

All this working out makes me exhausted. When I lived in the city, I never saw anyone go for a run outside, at least not in my neighborhood. I mean, we would run out for a smoke, a drink, a coffee, but actual running was not on the list. So here I am, bored to death in suburban animal kingdom hell. I am to get healthy. I get a gym membership. Ugh, come on! Makeup, ladies? Really? It is bad for your pores, and I have adult acne as it is. A sports bra—no shirt. Really? I am a bowl full of jelly, and you are going to just wear a bra. I cannot take it. So, I go and have to stare at these ladies. Yes, they worked hard for their body. Congratulations, you are women, and we hear you roar, but I am like that weird aunt, so if you do not mind.

I build up a little, go from elliptical to treadmill, and I am feeling great. Fastest and longest run to date. I hop off, get some water. Fuck, I forgot to turn it off. "I am being dragged like roadkill. "OMG, help me!"

"This is the worst day ever. They should have a sign that says, *Dumbass, turn off the machine.* So, guy comes to my aide and pulls me off the "dreadmill." I am totally embarrassed, and the new kid working the front desk wants to call 911. I have blood coming from my head, arm, and leg. I turn to the kid. "Don't you fucking dare call 911."

I never did see that kid again. I am surprised people did not pull their phones out and start videoing it. Fuck. Note to self: Check YouTube. I laugh about it but hey, just another reason to hate suburban life. WORKOUT FREAKS!

How are all these moms so fit? What do they do all day? I know, eat, clean, yadda, yadda, but boring. I love my Mediterranean curves. I am okay with it. Plus, did you see all the fucking animals out here? I am starting a safari tour guide in my area if you want to check it out.

I am part of a running group. Me! Do you believe it? The not-fit smoker. I have not been a member exceptionally long. I call myself the "honorary member." You know, so I can still go to the parties and lunches. Do not deny it, people, you love a good party!

Appetizers are my friend. I run a little with them. Fuck, I must quit. They get up at ass-crack early in the morning. Did you know that? It is dark out and, people, the skunks are still out. What is wrong with you people? I am running, and it's early morning (the first and only time this early), and there is a car following me and some girls. I mention how it has circled us four times. They did not notice. Of course, they did not. Rookies. I pick up a small stick. I am going to shank the guy with it if he tries to kidnap one of us. I am going to be prepared. I let them know that it is not safe, and they need to be aware, and if he comes again, we will put a plan of attack in place. Now, I find a really big stick. The stick will protect us. I will javelin it at him. Poke his eye out. Stab him in the throat. We will yell and run. Stay in pairs of two to get help if one of us gets grabbed. We got this, ladies! This fucker is going down. Well, turns out our stalker, or shall we call him the newspaper delivery man, was able to provide us with invaluable coupons. Thank you, Mr. Newspaper Delivery Man. Moral of the story is that you can never be too safe or have too many coupons.

The same newspaper delivery man would meet me again (must be fate) as I could not sleep, and I thought he was scouting out homes at four thirty a.m. Yes, I come from the city—I do not trust anyone.

Yay, I made a friend. Yep, this city girl made a suburban friend. She works out (and so did I for a crazy time). Honestly, I did not like her at first. Thinner than me, worked out better than me, stronger than me, lived in my town... what! Fuck, then let's run, bitch. I got this down. I am training for a marathon. She picks a hill. Oh, it's on you, mother! She helped me complete my first marathon, and I love her to death. We laugh about it now because she felt the same way about me. Girls are silly.

Self-esteem issues at forty, come on. Well, she is forty; I am younger. Old hag!

Those working out days were great, and I was in tip-top condition. So, ask me why I don't do it so much anymore? Well, I was attacked by a coyote... nah, just kidding. Working out got me a hemangioma on my liver. Basically, I got fucked!

Going to the hospital thinking you are having a heart attack is no fun. I ran out of the house. The newspaper delivery man drove me. Just kidding. Turns out I needed surgery. Blah, blah, totally suburban fine (was it the suburban water? OMG stop it! I am kidding; it was all the porn I started watching).

Okay, so in hospital, had surgery—fall in hallway. DRUGS! Say it loud. Drugs are your friend when you are in pain! Drugs are your friend. (I do not condone drug abuse, and this is a fake book, people. Fake as in not real. Okay, somewhat fake, ha-ha... or is it?)

Shot! La-la land ensues. I wake up at three a.m. and look around. Okay, I know I am in the hospital, but for what? Boob job? Nope. Tummy tuck? Possible, but it hurts like hell. Fuck! What is my name? Why can't I think of my name? Where is that fucking button?

"Yes, can I help you?"

"Sure, what's my name, and why am I here?"

"We will be right in."

Let me tell you—when a nurse tells you that you are married, but you do not remember, your first thought is, *Fuck, I am wasting a good opportunity here.* I obviously got my memory back. It was good while it lasted. In the hospital for weeks, and it sucks. No cute doctors. It is sad. There should be some sort of mandate, like possible dying patient—bring in the hot doctor. My stay was fine except for the "wagging finger" incident, as I like to call it. So here it is. It's a good story, and you will appreciate it and never look me in the eye ever again.

Drugs make you constipated. See, I could never do drugs because I do not like needles, and I do not like to smoke any more, and well, frankly, I like my teeth. I mean, sure, I would be skinny, but no teeth? People, I am a foodie, and I need teeth. Itching would drive me crazy. Skinny does not matter to me, especially when you are one hot piece of ass like myself! Are you following along? Pros: Skinny. Cons: No teeth, bad skin, no teeth.

Back to the wagging finger.

So I am constipated. If you have ever been severely constipated, then you know that this is no joke. It is so painful you cannot imagine. After screaming for four hours trying to poop (yes, it is such a dirty word), I receive my options. First option is the wagging finger to be stuck in my ass. Are you fucking kidding me? Yes, this is an option. It is not even my own finger. It is the poor nurse that would have to do it. I am so impacted that my ass just might eat her finger. It could be lost for days. Have you seen the size of my ass? Second option is a suppository. Okay, not too bad, but it will not do the trick. Third option: Enema. I went with option three. Not going to lie; it was humiliating. Not going to lie; it was disgusting. Not going to lie; it felt wonderful. Alleluia! Alleluia! Alleluia! The angels have sung. I am singing. The heavens opened. To give you an idea of the relief I received, it took me one hour to clear out, over eight flushes, and the back-pressure relief, and the pain was gone. Nothing spells relief like getting water forced into your ass. Ahh! My poor husband. He was mortified, shocked, scared (but I was screaming in pain), but hell, it is not about him. Suck it up, buttercup!

And that, my friends, is my anthem if I were to have one. So, don't work out. It only leads to surgical issues and enemas. I am kidding; you know that comment is not true.

While all this hell was going on, I realized people living in the suburbs are really nice. People came and brought me dinners, walked me like a dog outside so I could get fresh air. I even had the luxury of getting waxed at home. You know, ladies, how nice it is when someone comes to your house and waxes your lip and eyebrows. You feel like a queen. I did not feel like a queen because being Italian and not being able to shave for six weeks due to blood thinners makes you look like Bigfoot. I am not exaggerating. (Of course I am, this whole damn book is an exaggeration.) You could braid my leg hairs, my arm hairs were a man's, and I had a unibrow and a mustache. I would walk around twirling the end of my mustache, saying, "How do you do?" You know you just read that in a man's voice with an accent and pretended I wore a top hat. Ugh. I cannot get to the salon. Okay, I hate the suburbs again! Fuck you, suburbs and your no sidewalk or curb area streets, fuck you! A wonderful salon owner in town comes with her waxing kit to help me out. Oh, how I love you, suburbs; you are wonderful. Oh my God, I feel like a woman again. Other than the fact that I look like a 1970s' porn star "down there", I am good! Feeling good, and ugh, fucking suburbs again.

So, while I was in hospital, some crazy suburban bitch decided to spread some crazy rumor about me (I maybe talked to her twice) and said she spoke to me while I was at the public pool swimming all summer. This is what is funny about suburban moms: They are liars and crazy. Not all of them, of course, but…

Dear Crazy Suburban Mom,

You are a liar! You are not a good person! GO FUCK YOURSELF!

Sincerely,
    Fucking Crazy City Girl turned Suburban Mom
    P.S. SUCK IT AND SUCK IT HARD

God, I feel so much better. This was actually funny to me. Where is that damn coyote when you need one? All is well, and I am getting my shit together to run around the animal kingdom again. Move over skunks, here I come. Fuck! Hernias! Not one, not two, not three, four. Yes, four hernias, due to the first surgery. I was in denial the first two months.

"It's crazy. I eat just a cracker, and this thing bulges out of my stomach."

"You are just depressed from everything that went on. But let us do an endoscopy and a colonoscopy just in case."

It is 2015, medical people. You cannot find better shit to drink? I mean, after gagging for a day and the next, really? Fucking step it up a notch.

"Results are negative. We think it's depression."

"So, you see my stomach now, right? I am biting into a cracker, and you see what it looks like now, right (it ballooned out), and this is depression?"

Are you fucking kidding me? I HATE THE SUBURBS. That shit would not go down in a city hospital. Long story short, finally surgery. Doctor gets delayed due to an emergency, fuck me, now I wait! I am okay with it as I feel he needed to warm up. Outpatient surgery—be home that night. Well, not if you have my luck. Shitty luck. The shitty five days in the hospital. Being in the hospital so much, you must make the most of it. I swear to God I am so lucky my husband took my purse home. Do you know what good shit they sell late at night? You can get a knife, pajamas that look like jeans, a pillow, and glasses, really anything. Speaking of which, I am still waiting for some shit to come.

The fun part of hospital stays is the catheter. Do you really think I am serious? My bladder was not working right away—they call it "being asleep"—so I had to be re-catheterized three times. That will hinder your sex drive for sure. Oh, and if that was not painful enough, they will send you home, and you will come back with an extremely painful UTI. FUCK THE SUBURBS.

I am here now. In the suburbs, not going anywhere any time soon. This place is growing on me. I actually end up liking the hospital; it is very nice. The old one I went to in the city was like a prison. They still had those old televisions where the channel actually rolls. Fuck you, city! No, I am just kidding. I love you, city. I love, love, love you.

During this time, I realized two things. There are really good people out there, and there are crazy bitches out there. I can get all sentimental on you all, stating that life is short, seize the day, but that is not funny, so spend, spend, spend, have a blast because fuck it, you're going to die anyway—might as well go out with a bang. That is not really proper advice, and I would not tell my kids that advice, but I don't have kids, so fuck you, do it. Okay, I have kids, but then it is not funny. I really did not appreciate my single or kid-less days. I should have traveled and seen the world.

Types of Women

Let's discuss the type of women you find in Suburbia, USA. We are going to start out with the worst of the worst. The self-righteous, I am better-than-everyone-else fucker! This person does not know how to shut the fuck up. Thinks she can say whatever she wants whenever she wants. She can dish it but cannot take it. She is nothing less than a waste. Here you have a woman who thinks she is better than everyone. She is a stay-at-home mom but does not have to be. She takes multiple naps throughout the day because she is, well... lazy. Now I am not saying I have not taken a good nap, but she makes it her job to take a nap. If she holds a job, she makes it known that she is the most important person at her job, and without her, there would be no such company.

She goes around talking about other women and yet acts like the same woman that she is talking about is her best friend. Damn, I would have loved to tell the one that is being talked about by you-know-who. I am not a fucking rat. So, this terrible person has terrible kids. I do not blame the kids. I mean, it is not their fault. Their

71

mother makes them want for nothing (which is not a bad thing), but they treat people with disdain and lie to get what they want. They are taught to sacrifice any type of moral or good nature for the sake of themselves. For their selfishness, their own quick satisfaction. It really is a shame. These poor, poor children will end up becoming the douchebags of the world. Again, I do not blame the kids. They are a product of their environment. It is sad, really. So this is bringing me down, down, down. I am going to move on now to the other mother. Oh wait, this person usually has a nice husband but, when with his wife, he does not have a pair of balls! All she does is belittle and berate her man—this poor guy. Okay, moving on.

The next type of woman is the worker mom. She goes outside the home and works while still maintaining a house. I fucking love these moms. Honestly, I do not know how they do it. Get themselves ready, get their kid (or kids) ready, get them to school. They go to work, they come home, they do homework, they cook dinner, they clean, they do laundry, they shop, they attend events. Shit, I am exhausted typing all this out. These women are 'Superwomen." I truly have the utmost respect for them. Even deeper respect if they are doing it alone, with no partner to help. These women are truly the nicest. They listen; they are honest and respectful. They do not have time to deal with petty nonsense, and that is why I love them. A no-bullshit approach. Perfect. Even as busy as they are, they make time for you because you are a friend, and they care.

Next, you have the part-time worker and stay-at-home mom. I envy these women. They can do it all. They have a good balance of work, home, and self-care. These ladies have it all. They are down-to-earth and are highly organized. There is really not too much to say about them. *Can you come and help me organize?*

Now, the next type of woman is the stay-at-home mom. (Insert dramatic music.) There are three types of stay-at-home moms. Type one is your regular stay-at-home mom. Type two is the PTA-all-involved-in-school mom, and type three is the batshit-crazy mom.

Let's' start out first with the regular stay-at-home mom. This mom can get bored, has a perfect house, volunteers a little (but not a ton), writes books (wink wink), and has a bittersweet love-hate relationship with the fucking 'burbs. This mom usually gets talked about by the crazy stay-at-home moms or by the self-righteous pieces of crap. See, they have nothing better to do and need to downgrade someone. The regular stay-at-home mom minds her business. She does not care what Person A said about Person B. She does not need to be your friend for the sake of being friends. She is a good person who is well rounded in family, friends, and most importantly, her children's lives. She wants the best for them without sacrificing self-respect or morals. She is a good person. Not just because she says it or thinks it but because she acts it.

Type two: The PTA-stay-at-home mom. She is involved in all school activities and usually boasts about how much she does. She wants the pat on the back, and she wants to make sure you know all she does. Now, before you get your fucking panties in a bunch, I know and you know this is not all, people. It is a fucking book; stop being so fucking politically nice. You look stupid.

Now, my favorite type of mother is up next. Of course, I have to round it off with the batshit-crazy-stay-at-home mom. She really is my favorite mom. She provides me with entertainment and the neighborhood with entertainment. You better believe that people fucking talk out here in Suburbia, USA. She is happy, smiley on the outside, waving hello, but then it comes. The clouds roll in and the sky gets dark and thunderous and crazy starts pouring down from the heavens. HA! I heard about it; I have seen it with my very own eyes. People are FUCKING CRAZY! I hate the suburbs. Let us talk about some of these stories. You will not believe me, but they are true. What is even better is that I bet some of the crazies read this and will think, *Hey, she is talking about me*. Probably not talking about you, but if you think that, then you are a batshit-crazy person. Accept it. Embrace it. Fucking go see a specialist! It is okay. You have seen it over the years. You have been a part of it. It's all true, and it's okay.

I just cannot get over people. Who gives someone the right to think they are better than anyone else? Dramatic people who love to put up a fight for every little fucking thing. That is what this world has come to... everyone bitching and complaining. There is no compassion in the world.

"I'm sorry, my daughter's teacher gave her a green folder. Do you believe it? I am so offended! My daughter loves blue, and he gave her green, and I am totally offended. I am writing to him right now! Off to all the parents on the Facebook parent site, the school chat room, the school website." What a joke!

"Billy was mean to Jessica because Billy was playing with all his boy friends on the playground, and they said there was no room in the game for Jessica to play. I am emailing his parents." *Um, really?* Bros before hoes. I mean, give me a fucking break. People, shut the fuck up!

I got a great one for you. Let us talk fundraisers. Fundraisers are optional! You absolutely do not have to do them. You have a choice to participate or not to participate. That is it! That is the bottom line. It is simple; it is a choice. You do not have a right to bitch about an optional program. It is raising money for our kids. If you try, you can actually give a negative about all fundraisers. Books exploit children to buy crap like posters or chocolate calculators; coffee cake ones are not healthy; candle ones run the risk of fires... do you get my point? Shut up and do not participate in them if you do not like them. Better yet, do not bitch about something that you had a choice to participate in. Okay, okay, so here is the story.

Hot lunch day fundraiser in which you can choose to participate. Your kid gets something like a hot dog, chips, cookies, juice box. Healthy? No. But it is a fundraiser, and it is optional. Again, optional.

Parent Self-righteous says, "Our kids should be getting a healthy snack like apples and carrots." *Um, hello, it's optional.*

Parent Self-righteous says, "Why are our kids not getting this for hot lunch?" *Um, hello, it is optional.* It is a fundraiser to raise money. You do not have to participate.

Parent Self-righteous says, "I would have been on the committee, but I do not have time with all the kids' activities." *Hold up! Are you fucking kidding me?*

This is everyone's life. Every parent. Who the fuck do you think you are? So, you are better than all the other parents and busier than all the other parents? Parent Self-righteous does not let the healthy treat option go. Keeps hounding about this fundraiser that now the board wants to drop this fundraiser. Over ten thousand dollars was donated to the school due to this fundraiser, and now this lazy, self-righteous bitch is going to cause this to happen. It is a fucking fundraiser that you do not have to participate in! Do not buy the optional fun hot lunch for your kid. STUPID! STUPID! STUPID! Oh, and she is so stupid that she does not realize that a five-dollar hot lunch will then become an eight-dollar hot lunch... and people bitched at the five-dollar price. This is what is great about this country. You can talk out of your ass, and hey, it is okay—free country. The people who head up these fundraisers are saints. They have to put up with parental bullshit, and I give them praise. If you are going to bitch about a program, then head it up. You do not have a right, and you look like an asshole, although you probably are, so there's that. This is why being nice to dumbass people is so hard. What you really want to do is stand up and say, "Shut up, dumbass." Do not buy it for your kid and be done.

I am not saying that all heads of committees are perfect either. I love the "I am the boss" type. They have no respect for parent or student volunteers. They want it their way or no way. They suck! I would love to go up to these moms and say, "You are a fucking controlling bitch! These are volunteer parents and kids that are excited to help. Shame on you." Fucking suburbia.

This parent does not want kids (like eighth-grade kids) to help because, well, there is no reason; she is just a controlling bitch. When an eighth-grader wants to help pass out cake at a musical recital, you let them. You do not say no for their own recital. Controlling bitch, I feel bad for your kids. This is the same parent that says, "My kid, my kid, my kid." Well, wait. What about *my* kid? Or *her* kid? Or the community's kids? Swear these parents have a sense of entitlement. How the fuck were they raised, and where the fuck were they raised? You should probably homeschool your kid and have no contact with the outside world because, well, frankly, you are a self-righteous problem-causing bitch. You are not here to make things better. You are not here to improve the schools. You are not here to help the children. You are not here to watch our children better themselves. You are not here to watch the children become successful. You are not here to advance. You are here to be a bitch. You are here to be controlling. You are here to have it your way or no way. You are not a good person. Remember, just because you call yourself a good person does not make you one. You have a false sense of reality on life. You are what is wrong with the world today. You should look in a mirror because you are the first to throw stones. You have no real problem-solving skills but just like to bitch and bitch and bitch. Your sense of entitlement is disgusting, and your sense of situational handling is poor. Your "iron fist" and "opinionated speech" lacks depth, thought, or education. Oh, and by the way, just because you do have a degree does not make you smart or educated. You lack compassion and people skills. You are why everyone in the world is a pain in the ass. Your first-world problems are stupid. Your sense of entitlement is stupid. Your lack of being able to go with the flow or provide any real dialogue is ridiculous. You are the first person when someone disagrees with you to say you are being attacked. Nope, you are just a self-righteous mom who thinks her shit does not stink. Oh, and by the way, it does! Everyone can smell it a mile away. I fucking hate Suburbia, USA. I swear if someone told me that there was a town that raised people like this, I would be like, "That figures." The kids all think they are winners, and they are not. This "everyone gets a medal" is stupid. There are audience members for a reason. Not everyone is good at everything.

Friendships and Marijuana

I think it's funny that growing up as a kid, you used to have to hide all the pot smoking you did. Now you have it wide out in the open, and as forty-something-year-old's, you are hiding it from your kids now. It is a little insane to me that you can actually go buy it and smoke it legally, I guess. You have a bunch of middle-aged men and women running around Suburbia going to dispensaries like candy stores buying edibles, hiding from their children, getting high. It's like an episode from the *Twilight Zone*. If our parents truly knew what was going on, they would have thought the world would have lost its mind.

You have your four types of marijuana parent smokers. There's the pressured smoker who will try it but does not really do it and does it because everyone else is doing it. I feel bad for this person. Honestly, they are awkward and usually end the night early. Then there is the child that usually is the "OMG-I-am-so-high"-and-will-not-shut-up-about-it person. There is the you-did-not-even-know-they-did-it person. Not too much to say about this person; they keep their mouth shut and move on. Lastly, there is the polite you-want-some smoker and move on. All these smoker's kind of seem like they just started, had a midlife crisis, and need something in their life, and since it became legal and since cigarettes kill, this is what they chose.

Friendships are tricky because only your closest of the closest know that you do it—the stigma of actually smoking it. And in the suburbs, having friends is super tricky. It makes it funny watching them hide from their kids and parents and jump into bushes.

Girlfriends

Let me put it out there. Girlfriends are the worst. Yes, it is a love-hate relationship. I do not care if you are fifteen, twenty-two, or forty-five. It is all the same bullshit. We are all crazy motherfuckers. You can say you are not. You are. You can say you are a good friend. Okay, you probably are, but you probably are not too. Rule of advice: If you did not hear it with your own ears and did not see it with your own eyes, then shut the FUCK UP. I mean, this is good, solid advice. There are so many types of girlfriends. Let me give you a quick and brief description.

The Through Thick and Thin: This friend will go to bat for you. She will be by your side no matter what. She will always be there and will always be your friend no matter your situation—poor, rich, single, married.

The Loyalty: She has your back and can think on her feet.

The Stalker: You are her only friend and can only be her friend and no one else's. She will hunt you down if you make another friend and is batshit crazy. You will not realize this until it is too late.

The Clique: They are like the stalker but in a pack, and like the stalker, you will not realize this until it is too late.

The Normals: Just regular people who wish you well. (Holy shit, there are people out there like this!)

There are batshit-crazy friends out there that will track your whereabouts to see when you pulled into your driveway; give a shit if you liked their Facebook post.

There will be friends who will not be there for you when you need them most. But there will be that one friend who will be there for you. Who you can call, and you can talk to? She may be from the city, she may be from the suburbs, she may be dressed in a Victorian gown, and you met her in your basement during a storm. Nah, I'm just fucking with you. Whoever that fucked up friend is of yours, cheers to your fucking crazy-ass life!

What I Learned

So all these experiences have made me a better person. I am at an age now that, really, I let a lot more slide off my back. I think everybody reaches a point in their life when this happens. Clothes do not matter, how my house looks, the car I drive (and yes, it is still a minivan) … you get the point. Here is what does matter to me: My wonderful family. That, is it! My kids, my parents, my husband, my brothers and sisters. Friends come and go. The good non-judgmental ones stay by your side, and the others pass into the night. This is not a bad thing, just life. As I have gotten older, my friend list has dwindled. I am much pickier and more reserved. Not everyone has to like me, and I do not need to be friends with everyone. I will be cordial to you, especially if you are one of these suburban fucks that thinks that they are better than everyone. I do not hate you. I do feel sorry for you. My family means the world to me. I will strive for them and thrive because of them, the good and the bad.

I have also learned that people are assholes. Yes, they are out there in the world making bullshit up to appease their poor souls. You cannot change these people. You cannot help these people. All you can do is smile. That will really piss them off.

I am in love with my husband. This, next to my children, is the best thing. He warms my heart. He keeps me going. He believes in me. He makes me want to punch him when he rolls his eyes. I love all these things about him. I am one of the fortunate that have gotten his love since we were young. I am one lucky duck. He makes me a better person. He is my calm! Kind of makes you want to puke, doesn't it? This lucky piece of ass has me for the rest of his life. Pretty damn lucky if you ask me.

Animals want to fuck with me. Yes, it is true. There is my conspiracy theory. I think they hold quarterly meetings to see what they can do to torture me. I do not know why I am so afraid of them. Are they too sneaky for me? They are probably smarter than me, and that is why I am so afraid.

Minivans rule! Do you know how much shit you can get into a minivan? If there were an apocalypse, you could live in a minivan. Do not knock the van. Bikes, bags, coolers, sixteen cup holders, a million kids. Put your sunglasses on and jam to some music, and off we go. Coolest MILFs and DILFs out there. Makes you want to go out and get one now, doesn't it? Go to the

Urban Dictionary if you do not know what a DILF is—okay, it's a Dad I'd Like to Fuck—you're welcome!

No two suburbs are the same.

People who live in the suburbs do not mind their own fucking business. I mean, really? People, worry about your own life. Why are you getting involved in other people's lives? Are you bored, lonely, hating your own life? Open your own closet first; that should keep you busy for the rest of your life.

Fad diets are an epidemic in Suburbia, USA. If one person starts a fad diet, everyone will be on it. No one wants another person to pass them up. It is so crazy. How about let us be happy for that person and encourage whatever they are trying regardless of how you feel about the specific diet. They are trying to better themselves. Why shun them or the diet? What did they or it ever do to you?

Clubs are bullshit. Book club, dinner club, wine club, card club, candy club, poker club. You name it, there is a club for it. Please let us call it what it is: I-need-to-get-out-of-the-house-without-the-kid's club. Therefore, leaving the other adult at home to finish homework, baths, bedtime, pack lunch (okay, that usually does not happen), clean up. (This does not happen either.)

Small suburbs usually mean close-knit family ties are in the community. So, do not talk shit about anyone because they are all related and will find out.

Do not talk shit if you do not want anyone to find out.

There is no loyalty among people in a small community. People are bored and just want to talk shit.

Never underestimate a pissed off mother whose kid just got picked on.

Not everyone is a bully.

There are good people in the world.

I adore my kids.

Golfing is a bullshit sport that is played just to get away.

Sparring is an actual thing.

Kids are overscheduled.

Dieting is never ending.

Wine is delicious and a savior.

Your car will smell like fast food for days, so just cook.

Hire people to do work around your house. It will be done right, save time for you and your hubby. Think of it as you are supporting the economy, and it will save your marriage.

Kids are cute.

Kids are assholes.

Not all parents raise their kids to be good people. These parents usually think they raised good kids but do not even know the truth because they are blind from the get-go.

Coffee is a must to survive.

There is a food pantry in your neighborhood; go find it and donate.

Raising a family is fun, challenging, exciting, and exhausting.

I love my kids unconditionally. They make my world sing, and that is all I need.

I love life and the mess it brings.

To my loves, my sons, Michael and Matthew.

Running a marathon – my first and last

Liver surgery: defeated death